YOUR TONGUE CAN TELL

DISCOVER YOUR SENSE OF

VICKI COBB

Illustrations by
Cynthia C. Lewis

THE MILLBROOK PRESS
BROOKFIELD, CONNECTICUT

The author takes full responsibility for the accuracy of the text, and gratefully acknowledges Marcia Pelchat, Ph.D., and Pam Dalton, Ph.D., of the Monell Chemical Senses Center for their creative contributions and review of portions of the manuscript.

Published by The Millbrook Press, Inc.
2 Old New Milford Road
Brookfield, CT 06804
www.millbrookpress.com
Library of Congress Cataloging-in-Publication Data
Cobb, Vicki.
Your tongue can tell: discover your sense of taste / Vicki Cobb;
pictures by Cynthia C. Lewis.
p. cm. —(The five senses)
Summary: Text and suggested activities explore the sense of taste,
how it works, and how it can help us detect which foods are sweet,
sour, salty, or spicy.

ISBN 0-7613-1473-3 (lib. bdg.)

1. Taste—Juvenile literature. [1. Taste. 2. Senses and sensation.]
I. Lewis, Cynthia Copeland, 1960– ill. II. Title.
QP456.C625   2000   612.8'7—dc21   99-047873

Ever chew on cardboard? Yuck! Probably not. Cardboard doesn't taste good, so we don't eat it. This is a good thing, because cardboard is not food. But what if your food tasted like cardboard? You probably wouldn't want to eat. And if you didn't eat, you'd starve. So being able to taste is important for staying alive.

Scientists study the way we taste things. They ask questions that can be answered by doing experiments. You can be a scientist, too. When you do the experiments in this book, you'll make exciting discoveries about taste.

Dinner prepared by a mother who can't taste.

Eat up, kids! There's paper bag pudding for dessert!

What part of your body do you taste with? Look in a mirror. Stick out your tongue. See the tiny bumps that cover it? They are called *taste buds*. Can you guess why? Do they look like little unopened flowers? Take a closer look with a magnifying glass. Check out other people's tongues as well.

Taste buds are full of nerves that send messages to your brain. Your brain tells you what you're tasting.

You have about 3,000 taste buds on your tongue. Different kinds of taste buds send different chemical messages.

THIS TASTE IS SWEET

Put a pinch of sugar on your tongue. How does it taste? Sweetness is a taste that makes you smile. It tastes good, and that's important. Human milk is very sweet, much sweeter than cow's milk. Sweetness is a taste that babies love, and babies must love milk if they are going to thrive and grow.

MOLLY, MISUNDERSTOOD   By Cindy Lewis

Does your whole tongue taste sweetness? Do an experiment to find out. You will need some honey and a toothpick. Dip the toothpick in the honey. Touch the tip of the honey-dipped toothpick to the middle of your tongue. Taste anything? Dip it again and touch it to the tip of your tongue. Try the underside of your tongue. Surprise! There are only certain areas on your tongue where you taste sweetness. Only certain taste buds are the sweetness detectors.

Can you smell sweetness? Sniff the sugar in a sugar bowl. Hold your nose while you taste candy, syrup, and apples. Do they still taste sweet? Tasting sweetness doesn't depend on your nose. Your sense of smell helps you tell the difference between the flavors of many sweet things—between apples and pears, for example. But you need only your tongue to detect sweetness. How many sweet things can you name?

Sweets have been a favorite of people since ancient times. In ancient times, people ate lots of fruit and honey.

Egyptian royalty mixed honey with dates for a really sweet treat. Chop up some dates, add some honey, and spread it on crackers. Then pretend that you are King Tut or Queen Nefertiti.

The white sugar in your sugar bowl comes either from a tall grasslike plant called *sugarcane* or from white roots called *sugarbeets*. When sugarcane and sugarbeets are processed in factories, the end result is pure sugar, in tiny shapes called *crystals*. Look closely at some sugar crystals with a magnifying glass. Are they all pretty much the same shape? Can you draw a sugar crystal?

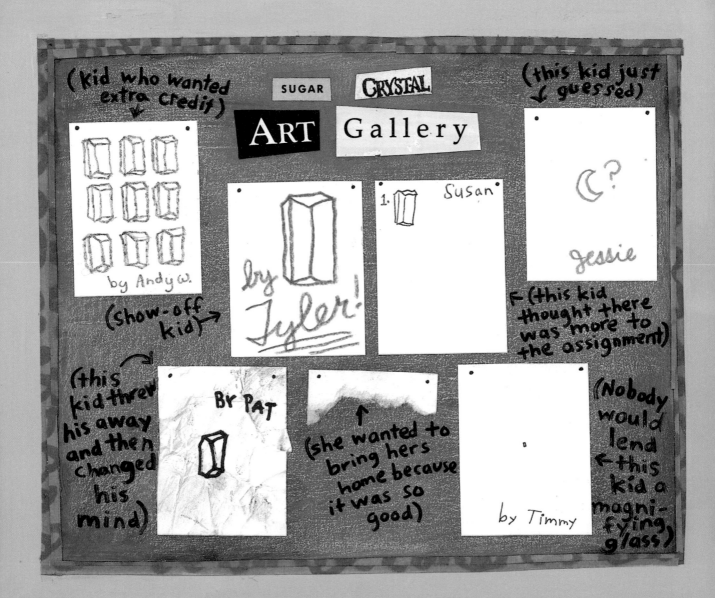

Large sugar crystals are rock candy. You can make some, but you must have a grown-up to help you. You will be using the stove and boiling hot liquid, which can be dangerous.

4   aluminum foil cupcake/muffin cups   small saucepan
½   cup water   wooden spoon
1   cup sugar   a grown-up

Put the sugar and water in a saucepan. Stir while heating over medium heat. The mixture will be cloudy. Bring it to a boil and let it boil for one minute after the liquid clears. Pour it into the four aluminum cups. After the liquid cools, move the cups to a place where they will not be disturbed. Sugar crystals will start to form by the next day. It can take several weeks for your rock-candy crystals to grow. From time to time, carefully remove the crust of crystals that forms at the surface. You can eat this crust. Look at the shape of a rock-candy crystal. Does it look like the shape of a crystal in your sugar bowl?

(Don't forget the grown-up!)

← stuff you'll need →

KISS the JUGGLING COOK

Your mouth can change something that's not sweet into something that is sweet. Do an experiment to see how. Chew on a plain soda cracker. At first it doesn't taste sweet at all. Get it good and gooey and hold it in your mouth. After a while it will taste sweet.

Here's why. Your saliva has a chemical in it that changes the starch in the cracker into sugar. Sugar goes directly into your bloodstream where its energy is used by your body. But starchy foods have to be digested—broken down into sugar— before they can enter your blood. This digestion starts in your mouth when you chew starchy food and mix it well with saliva. Usually you swallow the cracker before you give yourself enough time to taste the change.

THIS TASTE IS SALTy

Ever lick a sweaty upper lip? Ever taste your tears? How do they taste? Salty, that's how. Salt is in your tears, your sweat, your blood, your urine, even your saliva. When you don't have enough salt you may feel very tired and have muscle cramps. When you have too much salt you become very thirsty. Your amazing body makes sure that you have the right amount of salt without your having to think about it.

Even if you eat lots of pickles, pretzels, potato chips, and salted peanuts, your body gets rid of the extra salt automatically through sweat and urine. Salty foods taste good because you need to replace the salt your body gets rid of every day. But you don't need very much salt to stay healthy. A pinch of salt a day will do.

← uh-oh! She had more than a pinch!

PLA
Dry R
pea

Where on your tongue do you taste salt? Do an experiment to find out. Pour some salt into a small dish. Wet a clean toothpick and dip the wet end in the salt. Touch the salted toothpick to the middle of your tongue. Taste anything? Dip again and try another spot. What part of your tongue is the best salt taster? Is this the same part that tasted sweet? Are there any spots where you can't taste salt at all?

Help a grown-up prepare a meal without any salt. Eat mashed potatoes, plain boiled vegetables, and a plain broiled hamburger or chicken without any salt. Some people have to live on a salt-free diet. Do you think you would like it? When you've had enough salt-free food, sprinkle some salt on the rest of your meal.

Salt, like sugar, also forms crystals. Are salt crystals the same shape as sugar crystals? Look at some with a magnifying glass and find out for yourself. Now can you tell the difference between salt and sugar without tasting them?

Whaddya think? Sugar or salt? QUICK! GUESS!

I think I'm in the wrong book!

You can actually take salt crystals out of salty liquids. Put some pickle juice on a saucer that is any color but white. Let the water evaporate. This may take several days. With a magnifying glass, look at the crystals left behind when the plate is dry Are they the same shape as the salt crystals in your salt shaker? If you've ever been to the ocean, you already know one way to collect salt from seawater. Your skin becomes gritty with dried salt after the water evaporates.

Pickle Juice experiment in progress! DO NOT WASH PLATE!

The ocean is about as salty as your blood, sweat, and tears. In fact, the blood and body fluids of all animals have about the same percentage of salt as seawater. You wouldn't need to eat salt if you only ate meat and fish. Plant-eating animals, like deer, need to eat salt. They will travel for miles to find salt licks. Some people put out blocks of salt for animals. But there are many natural salt licks where, over millions of years, seas have dried up and left behind great deposits of rock salt. They are a good place for nature lovers to view wildlife.

I *TOLD* you deer don't come looking for salt, Fred! Pass me some chips, will ya?

Natural Salt Lick

Man, this is a drag! I can't WAIT until someone invents refrigerators!

Never mind REFRIGERATORS-- what about GO-CARTS and SATURDAY MORNING CARTOONS?

big barrels for the storage of salted meat were excavated from tree trunks three feet across.

spread codfish on the rocks to be dried by the sun. then salt them and pack them into barrels.

Before there were refrigerators, people used salt to keep meat and fish from spoiling. Meat and fish don't spoil if they are salted and dried. Salting makes the fluid come out of meat and fish so that the inside can be dried as well as the surface. You can buy tasty strips of dried beef called beef jerky. Dried salted codfish is very tough and much too salty to eat. But it will keep without refrigeration for months. In order to eat it, however, you must get rid of the salt by soaking it for two days and changing the water every few hours.

I'm still wa-a-ay too tough for you, fella. You're gonna hafta soak me a LITTLE longer... heh, heh, heh...

THIS taSte is sour

Ever suck on a lemon? Look in the mirror while you do it. Sourness is not a pleasant taste. Everyone who tastes something sour makes the same face. What tastes sour besides lemons? Unripe fruit is sour, and it can upset your stomach.

Its sour taste protects us from eating it. As fruit ripens, it also becomes sweet. Sweet and sour together make a taste we call *tart* that some people like. Taste some sour and tart foods. Try juices, rhubarb pie, salad dressing, sour cream, sourball candy, sweet-and-sour meatballs, pickles.

Where do you taste sourness on your tongue? Do an experiment to find out. Squeeze some lemon juice into a cup. Dip the end of a toothpick in the juice and touch it to a spot on your tongue. Test the middle of your tongue, the tip, and the sides. Try the inside of your cheek. By now you should know where your tongue tastes sourness best.

You can also tell if something is sour without tasting it. Here's how. Get a red cabbage. Have a grown-up help you chop up enough red cabbage to fill two measuring cups. Put the cabbage in a bowl and cover it with water. Let it soak for about ten minutes, then pour the mixture through a strainer so that you can collect the water. The water is now red, like the cabbage. Put about a tablespoon of the red cabbage juice in each of three small glasses. Add a teaspoon of orange juice to one glass. Add lemon juice and vinegar to the other glasses. What happens? Everything that has a sour taste will turn the red cabbage juice pink.

sour things that might turn the cabbage juice PINK

Sour lunch lady

lemon

Old Mrs. Bamberger's sour cat who hates everybody

Sour milk that Justin hid behind the sofa 2½ weeks ago because he hates milk

Sourness is caused by a kind of chemical called an *acid*. When acids are mixed with certain other substances, there is a chemical reaction such as the color change from red cabbage juice to pink. Can you change the red cabbage juice to another color? Put a tablespoon in a glass and add some baking soda. You get blue! Taste the baking-soda mixture. Is it sour? What happens when you add an acid to a blue cabbage-juice mixture? Can you turn it pink again?

Try making your own soda! Mix half a teaspoon of baking soda into orange or grapefruit juice, both acids. Ta-da! Bubbles! The bubbles are made of a gas called carbon dioxide. Drink your homemade soda and let the bubbles tickle your tongue.

this TASTE IS bitter

Ever bite into a square of baking chocolate? One unpleasant surprise. Instead of a wonderful treat, you tasted something so bitter you probably spit it out. Bitter is not a pleasant taste. Everyone makes the same terrible face when they taste it. Here's a list of some bitter things: the white part of grapefruit skin, unsweetened cocoa, instant-coffee grains . . . baking chocolate!

Clayton plays a mean trick on little Eddie...

Where do you taste bitterness on your tongue? Pour about a teaspoon of unsweetened cocoa into a dish. Dip a wet toothpick onto the cocoa and touch it to parts of your tongue. What do you taste with the tip of your tongue? How about testing the back of your tongue? Many of the taste buds for bitter are on the back of the tongue, the last place food goes before you swallow.

Many poisonous plants have a bitter taste. So our dislike of bitterness could protect us. Also, since we taste bitterness on the back of the tongue, we could spit out a bitter poisonous plant before we swallowed it.

However, not all bitter foods are poisonous. We even learn to like some bitter tastes, like coffee, if they are not too strong. Here are some partly bitter foods you might like: bittersweet chocolate, celery root, endive, radicchio (a red lettuce), Greek olives, quinine water (tonic).

Do you like chocolate? If you do, you're not alone. Chocolate is an all-time favorite flavor. The people who discovered chocolate were the Mayan and Aztec Indians of Mexico. They dried and roasted the beans of the cacao plant, then ground them up and cooked them with water. They served the mixture as a cold, thick, rich drink. Montezuma, an Aztec king, drank it out of a golden goblet and then threw the goblet into a lake. Scientists have found many golden goblets at the bottom of the lake. The Aztecs believed that this drink was a gift from the gods and very healthful. So they drank a lot of it.

The God of Chocolate

When the Spanish first came to Mexico almost five hundred years ago, they were served this favorite drink of the native people. They didn't like it very much because it was much too bitter.

But they took it back to Spain and someone had the great idea of mixing it with sugar. The sweetened chocolate was so delicious that some people thought it was sinful. But people couldn't stay away from it, and soon there were chocolate drinkers all over Europe.

Chocolate candy was invented by the Swiss a little more than a hundred years ago. They figured out how to make sweetened chocolate into firm little cakes. Chocolate candy is very different from the bitter bean it comes from. What a wonderful invention! Can you imagine living without it?

This taste is SPICY HOT or MINTY COOL

Take a bite of a chip with salsa on it. The heat comes from a spice called chili pepper or chili powder, a funny name for a spice that's not "chilly" at all. Chili powder is made from chili peppers, and they are both used to make food "hot." Chili can make your eyes water and your nose run. But it is full of vitamins and even kills some germs, so it is not bad for you to eat. Hold your nose as you eat the salsa. Can you feel its hotness?

Chilly Food

Chili Food

Can I have seconds?

Spicy hot is not really a taste. It is more like an irritation or pain, so you don't use your tongue to "taste" chili. Your tongue feels it. Your wrist can feel it, too. Put a few drops of Tabasco sauce on your wrist. Wait a few minutes. Does you wrist start to feel warm? Wash off the sauce, and the feeling goes away. The chili fires the same nerves in your skin that normally sense heat. So you are fooled into feeling something as hot that is not.

Your tongue has the same nerves to detect heat that your skin has. Chili fires these nerves, not taste buds. Chili burns more in your mouth than on your wrist because the skin in your mouth is wet and much more sensitive than dry skin. You must be careful not to get chili in your eyes or in a cut, where it can really hurt! When people cook with chili peppers, they need to keep their hands away from their faces.

After a nice, big chili dinner, Benny cooks his own dessert.

Christopher Columbus tasted chili when he arrived on the Caribbean islands, and he brought it back to Spain. The people of Europe didn't like its burning taste, but spice traders brought it to other parts of the world. The people in the Middle East, India, and Africa loved it. Chili peppers are used in the foods of India, Africa, China, and Mexico, among others.

Want to feel something cool on your tongue that's not really cool? Hold your nose and swish some peppermint mouthwash. Can you taste the minty flavor? Let go of your nose. Now can you taste the mint? Hold your nose again and breathe through your mouth while you wait a few minutes. Does your mouth start to feel cool? Your tongue has nerves to detect coolness. These are different from the nerves that detect heat. Something in the mouthwash fires these nerves, and you feel coolness that's not really there.

The peppermint plant contains a chemical called menthol. Menthol is put into cough drops and ointments, among other things. Can you name some cool treats? How about chewing gum and peppermint candy? Try some and see.

Close-up view of the nerves in your tongue detecting coolness...

COOL   COOL   COOL

One Last Taste

Scientists used to believe that the tongue tasted four tastes: sweet, salty, sour, and bitter. But there may be a fifth taste that your tongue can detect. It is described as meaty and slightly salty and delicious. It is found in many Japanese and Chinese dishes. The Japanese call this taste *umami,* or "wonderful taste." It has the chemical name of monosodium glutamate, or MSG. You can buy it in the supermarket as Accént®.

Many people are allergic to MSG. If you have a bad reaction to Chinese food, which usually has MSG in it, don't try this experiment. Hold your nose and sprinkle some MSG on your tongue. What do you taste? Have the cook in your house make some chicken soup. Eat some without MSG. Then add some MSG. Can you taste the difference?

SWEET TREATS are EVERYONE'S favorite! After all, WHO would choke down spinach if there wasn't chocolate cake for dessert?

Without a pile of salty chips, Sandwiches would be VERY lonely.

HEY! When salt makes people thirsty, what do they crave? LEMONADE! That's what! SOUR POWER!

You're ALL wrong! Everyone knows BITTER IS BETTER!

How come THOSE FOUR get all the attention?

Now you have had a taste of taste. What did you learn? Wherever there are taste buds there are receptors for all tastes. But your sense of taste is also affected by your other senses. How would you like to eat with your nose stuffed up all the time? How does an onion taste when you hold your nose? How important is the texture of a food—its mushiness or crunchiness? How important is its temperature? Taste is only part of the total experience of food. Can you dream up your own experiments with taste? It's something to think about the next time you eat.

I have just proven that CUPCAKES taste better than EAR WAX! A SCIENTIFIC BREAKTHROUGH!

Woof

ABOUT THE AUTHOR

Vicki Cobb thinks she has an excellent sense of taste. That's why she picks such fun things to write about. When she finished writing this book, she had learned that it is more fun to taste things than it is to think about tasting them! You can visit Vicki at www.vickicobb.com

ABOUT THE ILLUSTRATOR

Cindy Lewis had the good taste to accept the job of illustrating this book. She has also shown her good taste in choosing her wonderful husband, Tom, and raising her three wonderful kids.